Pollution

Examining Cause and
Effect Relationships

Curriculum Consultant: JoAnne Buggey, Ph.D.
College of Education, University of Minnesota

By Robert Anderson

Greenhaven Press, Inc.
Post Office Box 289009
San Diego, CA 92198-9009

Titles in the opposing viewpoints juniors series:

Advertising
AIDS
Alcohol
Animal Rights
Causes of Crime
Child Abuse
Christopher Columbus
Death Penalty
Drugs and Sports
Elections
Endangered Species

The Environment
Forests
Free Speech
Garbage
Gun Control
The Homeless
Immigration
Nuclear Power
The Palestinian Conflict
Patriotism
Pollution

Population
Poverty
Prisons
Smoking
Television
Toxic Wastes
The U.S. Constitution
The War on Drugs
Working Mothers
Zoos

Cover photo: © 1991/Mark Ludak/Impact Visuals

Library of Congress Cataloging-in-Publication Data

Anderson, Bob, 1950-
   Pollution: examining cause and effect relationships / by Robert
Anderson ; curriculum consultant, JoAnne Buggey.
    p. cm. — (Opposing viewpoints juniors)
   Includes bibliographical references and index.
   Summary: Presents opposing viewpoints on pollution and its effects
on the atmosphere, water, and people of the planet.
   ISBN 0-89908-574-1 (alk. paper)
   1. Pollution—Environmental aspects—Juvenile literature.
[1. Pollution. 2. Critical thinking.] I. Buggey, JoAnne.
II. Title. III. Series.
TD196.C45A53 1992
363.73'2—dc20   92-25958
                                                         CIP
                                                          AC

CONTENTS

THE PURPOSE OF
THIS BOOK

An Introduction to
Opposing Viewpoints

When people disagree, it is hard to figure out who is right. You may decide one person is right just because the person is your friend or a relative. But this is not a very good reason to agree or disagree with someone. It is better if you try to understand why these people disagree. On what main points do they differ? Read or listen to each person's argument carefully. Separate the facts and opinions that each person presents. Finally, decide which argument best matches what you think. This process, examining an argument without emotion, is part of what critical thinking is all about.

This is not easy. Many things make it hard to understand and form opinions. People's values, ages, and experiences all influence the way they think. This is why learning to read and think critically is an invaluable skill.

Opposing Viewpoints Juniors books will help you learn and practice skills to improve your ability to read critically. By reading opposing views on an issue, you will become familiar with methods people use to attempt to convince you that their point of view is right. And you will learn to separate the authors' opinions from the facts they present.

Each Opposing Viewpoints Juniors book focuses on one critical thinking skill that will help you judge the views presented. Some of these skills are telling fact from opinion, recognizing propaganda techniques, and locating and analyzing the main idea. These skills will allow you to examine opposing viewpoints more easily. The viewpoints are placed in a running debate and are always placed with the pro view first.

Examining Cause and Effect Relationships

In this Opposing Viewpoints Juniors book, you will learn about the basic critical thinking skill of examining cause and effect. By learning how to identify cause and effect statements, you will be able to better evaluate the reasons authors give for their arguments.

A cause and effect statement claims that one thing causes another. Some examples of cause and effect statements are: Cigarette smoking causes lung cancer. She gets higher grades because she flatters the teacher. Pollution causes global warming. In each sample sentence, the writer tells about one thing (the cause) making something else happen (the effect).

Notice that some sentences can be proven to be true while others are mostly a matter of the writer's opinion. For example, many medical studies have shown that sentence 1 is true; there is a very strong cause and effect relationship between smoking and cancer. But sentence 2 might be harder to prove. There could be many reasons (causes) why "she gets high grades." The writer tells us one possible cause, but we would have to know a lot more about the situation before we could accept the writer's statement as true.

It is important to evaluate cause and effect statements. Just because an author tells us that one thing causes another thing to happen, it is not necessarily true. Some things to ask yourself when you are evaluating a cause and effect statement are: Does the statement seem logical? Does it make sense? Does the writer (or speaker) give any evidence to support the statement? If so, what kind of evidence is it? Some kinds of evidence are more reliable than others. A writer might use personal experience, scientific studies, opinions from experts, observations—the writer actually observes the thing happening—or several examples that all show the same relationship.

The authors of the viewpoints in this book take different stands on pollution. They disagree on the seriousness of pollution, the harm pollution causes, and who should regulate pollution. You will be asked to identify the causes and effects each author supplies to prove his argument. Next, you will be asked to analyze the cause and effect statements. For example, does the author's reasoning seem logical? Or are the causes and effects exaggerated or irrelevant? Finally, in the critical thinking activities at the end of every pair of viewpoints, you will be asked to determine which author presents the most logical causes and effects.

We asked two students their opinions about pollution. Examine their viewpoints. Look for examples of cause and effect in their arguments.

Pollution is a serious problem.

Every year, the earth becomes more polluted. One important reason for this is that the world's population is growing very fast. A larger population means more waste to dispose of. It also means more forest land must be cleared to support it. Many developing nations are industrializing, adding to air and water pollution.

Meanwhile, industrialized nations are creating even more poisonous chemicals. These chemicals pollute our air, water, and soil. They end up in our food and eventually in our bodies, where they make us sick.

If nations do not get pollution under control, the whole planet will get sick. There are signs that this is already happening. Global warming and a hole in the ozone layer of the atmosphere are changing the earth's climate. These changes are harming plants, animals, and humans. Reducing pollution is our only hope of saving the earth.

Pollution is not a serious problem.

Pollution is not a serious problem anymore. People now are more aware of the ecology. They are recycling and using products that do not add to pollution. Business and industry are finding ways to clean up pollution. They also have begun to provide products without polluting the environment.

Scientists are finding that global changes in climate and atmosphere happen, not because of pollution, but naturally. In addition, scientists have found that sulfur dioxide, a major air pollutant, reflects heat away from the earth, thus helping to prevent global warming.

Keeping the environment clean and healthy is a challenge. But people are meeting the challenge and conquering the pollution problem.

ANALYZING THE
SAMPLE VIEWPOINTS

Matthew and Marge have very different opinions about whether pollution is a serious problem. Both of them give examples of cause and effect arguments in their essays.

Matthew:

CAUSE	EFFECT
Growing population means more waste and deforestation.	More pollution.
Industrialized nations create chemicals that end up in our bodies.	People get sick.

Marge:

CAUSE	EFFECT
People are more aware of ecology.	They use nonpolluting products and recycle.
Business and industry are changing to help the environment.	They create products that do not pollute.

In this sample, Matthew and Marge express different beliefs about pollution. Both think they are right. Who do you think makes the most convincing argument? Why?

As you read the viewpoints in this book, keep a tally like the one above to compare the authors' arguments.

CHAPTER 1

PREFACE: Does Pollution Harm Earth's Atmosphere?

In 1984, scientists discovered a great hole in the ozone layer above the South Pole. In 1989, another, smaller hole was discovered above the North Pole. Because the ozone layer filters out much of the dangerous ultraviolet radiation from the sun, scientists were very concerned about the holes. If the holes grew bigger, it could mean earth would get much hotter. This would have drastic effects on the world's plants and animals.

To prevent these consequences, scientists looked for ways to stop the problem. Since the scientists knew that the element chlorine could break down ozone, they blamed the gases used in aerosol sprays for adding too much chlorine to the atmosphere. The aerosols were soon banned. Industries were ordered to stop using the gases, known as chlorofluorocarbons (CFCs). But the hole in the ozone did not shrink.

After more study, some scientists found that volcanic eruptions and other natural geological events spewed more chlorine into the atmosphere than all the aerosols ever used. Why, then, did the holes suddenly appear in the 1980s, if chlorine was the cause of them? Scientists could not answer this question, so many different theories developed. Environmentalists cried out for a ban on all CFCs and other ozone-eating chemicals. Industries protested the great cost of replacing such an inexpensive chemical without more proof that it was damaging the atmosphere.

Without the ozone layer, life on earth would not exist. But whether pollution is responsible for its erosion is hotly contested. The next two viewpoints debate this issue. They contain many cause and effect arguments. The questions in the margins of the viewpoints will help you examine cause and effect relationships.

Editor's Note: In this viewpoint, the author argues that air pollution is a serious problem because it threatens the whole planet. Air pollution contributes to global warming and weakens the ozone layer that protects the earth from too many ultraviolet rays. As you read, note the cause and effect arguments the author uses.

The author claims that air pollution causes damage to the earth's atmosphere.

According to Dr. Hansen, what causes the greenhouse effect?

Air pollution is damaging the earth's atmosphere. Large, smog-ridden cities exist in every area of the world, so air pollution is a worldwide problem. What makes air pollution even more serious is that it damages the whole planet. It causes the earth's atmosphere to warm up. It also eats away the atmosphere's protective ozone layer. These problems make air pollution an especially serious problem.

Global warming was first brought to the public's attention in 1988. In the United States, the summer of 1988 was one of the hottest and driest on record. In June of that year, Dr. James Hansen of the National Aeronautics and Space Administration (NASA) warned the U.S. Congress that the earth was getting warmer. Carbon dioxide (CO_2) and other gases were building up in the atmosphere, he said. These gases prevented heat from escaping into outer space. He called it the greenhouse effect, because the gases acted like a greenhouse, a glass building that holds in air heated by the sun. Hansen blamed the buildup of these "greenhouse gases" on the burning of petroleum-based fuels.

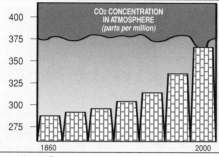

WORLD CARBON EMISSIONS

in billions of tons of carbon per year

World CO₂ emissions have steadily increased since the start of the Industrial Revolution.

CO₂ CONCENTRATION IN ATMOSPHERE (parts per million)

400
375
350
325
300
275

1860   2000

Source: *Beyond the Limits* by Donella Meadows, Dennis Meadows, and Jorgen Randers.

Global warming is dangerous because warmer temperatures can melt polar ice, raising sea levels and causing flooding. Warmer regions may dry out and become unproductive deserts. The only way to prevent such global warming is to decrease air pollution.

What effects may be caused by global warming, in the author's opinion?

Air pollution is also destroying the ozone layer that surrounds the planet. This layer absorbs a good deal of the sun's ultraviolet (UV) rays before they can reach the earth's surface. Without the ozone layer, a deadly amount of UV rays would strike the earth and the creatures that live on it.

What harmful effect on the atmosphere does the author claim air pollution causes?

Scientists know that certain chemicals called chlorofluorocarbons (CFCs) are escaping into the atmosphere and destroying the ozone layer. These chemicals are used in spray cans, air conditioners, refrigerators, Styrofoam, and many other products everywhere in the world. CFCs are no longer used in some products in the United States, but since they are inexpensive to use, industry does not want to replace them. As a result, CFCs are still part of a great many items manufactured throughout the world. Later research has also found that many other pollutants damage the ozone layer as well.

In the author's opinion, what is destroying the ozone layer?

Because of air pollution's role in weakening the ozone layer, more people are getting skin cancer. The U.S. Environmental Protection Agency (EPA) has calculated that for every 1 percent of ozone lost from the atmosphere the amount of UVs increases by 2 percent. This increase can cause an 8 percent rise in skin cancer rates. This means that nearly one hundred thousand more cases of skin cancer would occur every year in the United States alone.

The author cites statistics to support his argument that the destruction of the ozone causes what ill effect?

The pollution of the earth's atmosphere must be stopped. If it is not, life-giving air and sunshine may soon become earth's worst enemies.

A planetary threat?

The author argues that air pollution is a serious problem for the whole planet. What are two ways that air pollution endangers the earth? What effect does air pollution have on people's health, according to the author?

Pollution does not harm earth's atmosphere

Editor's Note: The author of this viewpoint argues that air pollution is not a threat to the earth's atmosphere. In fact, he argues, some pollution may help the atmosphere protect the earth. Watch for the author's cause and effect arguments.

The author uses many experts' opinions to support his cause and effect arguments. Do you think this makes his argument more convincing? Why or why not?

According to the author, why are CFCs not the cause of the hole in the ozone layer?

Is this cause and effect argument based on the author's opinion? Whose opinions are the basis of the argument?

What causes the hole in the ozone layer, according to Dr. McGrath?

According to the author, does pollution cause global warming? Why or why not?

Air pollution does not harm the earth's atmosphere. It neither destroys the ozone layer nor causes global warming. So argues professional meteorologist and aerospace engineer Dr. H. Read McGrath. "There is nothing we can release here [on the earth's surface] that can reach the ozone layer," says McGrath. He explains that a blanket of warm air prevents CFCs or other pollutants from rising into the ozone layer above the earth.

McGrath is not the only one to hold this position. Scientists at the Massachusetts Institute of Technology (MIT), England's Royal Meteorological Society, the National Oceanic and Atmospheric Administration, and other prominent research facilities agree.

Scientists have found that chlorine gas does break down ozone in the atmosphere, but only a small percentage of the chlorine released into the atmosphere comes from air pollution. Most of it comes from natural sources—sources that have been spewing chlorine into the air for millions of years. As geologist Rogelio Maduro points out, more chlorine is put into the atmosphere by volcanic eruptions, the evaporation of seawater, and many other natural phenomena than by CFCs and air pollution.

So why have scientists found holes in the ozone layer above the earth's polar regions? The sun's natural activity causes the holes, argues Dr. McGrath. McGrath claims that the sun goes through a regular cycle of intense activity for seven years followed by an eleven-year period of quiet. McGrath predicts the holes in the ozone layer will fill in after the seven-year period of solar activity ends in 1995.

Other scientists, like Gordon Dobson and NASA's Mark Schoeberl, believe the ozone hole is the result of natural changes in earth's weather patterns.

These weather variations are also most likely the cause of the recent warmer temperatures around the world. Some scientists, however, have argued that the earth is becoming unnaturally warmer. Environmentalists blame air pollution for global warming, but they are wrong. Scientists have been keeping records of earth's activities—like weather—for only about one hundred years. Despite the environmentalists' uproar, MIT scientists reported in 1989 that present temperatures are nearly the same as they were in the 1850s. In other words, global warming is a myth.

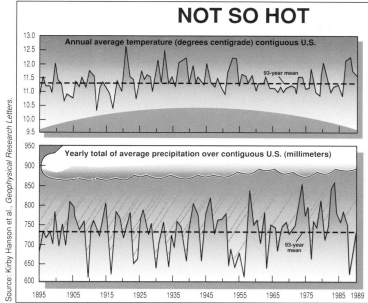

NOT SO HOT

Annual average temperature (degrees centigrade) contiguous U.S.

93-year mean

Yearly total of average precipitation over contiguous U.S. (millimeters)

93-year mean

Source: Kirby Hanson et al., *Geophysical Research Letters.*

The average temperature in the United States from 1895 to 1989 has been about 52 degrees Fahrenheit. The top graph shows that there have been hot and cold spells, but that a global warming trend has not been evident. The bottom graph shows the amount of rainfall during that same period. According to these data, the amount of rainfall is no less over a hundred-year period.

Environmentalists argue that carbon dioxide (CO_2) and sulfur dioxide (SO_2) are the causes of global warming. These gases are generated by, among other things, factories, electrical power companies, and automobiles. These sources of pollution may create smog in our cities, but they do not contribute to global warming. In fact, many scientists are now saying that sulfur dioxide may help prevent global warming. Researchers at the National Oceanic and Atmospheric Administration report that sulfur dioxide particles in the atmosphere create shiny clouds that reflect heat away from the earth.

In environmentalists' opinion, what causes global warming? Do any scientists disagree with this cause and effect argument? What is the scientists' opinion?

In the case of carbon dioxide, meteorologist McGrath states that it, too, may be helpful. It causes water vapor to condense in the atmosphere, he argues. This condensation helps keep a balanced temperature on earth.

According to the author's source, what effect does CO_2 have on the atmosphere?

These gases, condemned as atmospheric pollutants by environmentalists, are part of the earth's way of keeping its balance. And who knows better about what is good for the earth—the earth itself or environmentalists?

Good pollution?

The author mentions a certain pollutant that may help prevent global warming. What pollutant is it? How does it prevent global warming? Does this sound logical to you? Why or why not?

CRITICAL THINKING SKILL 1

Examining Cause and Effect

Viewpoints one and two offer different opinions on air pollution's effect on earth's atmosphere. In answering the margin questions, you have already thought about many of the causes and effects the viewpoints have presented. In this activity, you will review some of these and compare and contrast the author's reasoning.

Viewpoint 1:
Air pollution harms earth's atmosphere

CAUSE	EFFECT
buildup of greenhouse gases	global warming
release of CFCs into atmosphere	hole in ozone layer

Viewpoint 2:
Air pollution does not harm earth's atmosphere

CAUSE	EFFECT
SO_2 and CO_2 released into atmosphere	help prevent global warming
cycle of solar activity	hole in ozone layer that will fill in again later

Viewpoint 1 argues that air pollution harms the earth's atmosphere. What evidence does it present to prove that this is true? Does the viewpoint's conclusion seem logical? Why or why not?

Viewpoint 2 presents evidence to support the opposite conclusion. What is this evidence? Does the viewpoint's conclusion seem logical? Why or why not?

Which viewpoint do you believe presents the best case about air pollution's effect on earth's atmosphere? Why?

CHAPTER 2

PREFACE: Has Pollution Made Drinking Water Unsafe?

Environmentalists warn that groundwater is badly polluted. Environmental writer Steve Coffel calls groundwater pollution the plague of the 1990s because almost everyone uses groundwater and will be adversely affected if it becomes seriously polluted.

Groundwater is the water held beneath the earth in large pools and mineral formations. It is the largest available supply of drinkable water. Because groundwater collects at the lowest levels underground, pollutants that settle on the soil above ground or are buried in landfills eventually seep into it. Year after year they accumulate there. Some groundwater pollutants have been found in concentrations thousands of times greater than in surface water like lakes and rivers.

Those on the opposite side of the debate about water pollution contend that the water supply is safe. Researcher Kristine Napier, for example, argues that the public equates safe water with pure water and that the two are not the same. Napier points out that pure water has never existed in nature, only in laboratories. All natural water is contaminated by other ingredients. Whether it is safe to drink depends not so much on *what* is in it, but on *how much* of the contaminant is in it.

In addition, these people argue, water is tested much more thoroughly than in the past. Recent technology has allowed scientists to detect water pollutants at increasingly minute levels. When the scientists report their findings, the public becomes alarmed. But people have probably been drinking these small amounts of pollutants with their water for decades without ill effect. The presence of pollutants does not indicate danger, according to the American Council on Science and Health. It notes that the government has established levels of safety for all water contaminants. Contaminants in public water supplies are not allowed to exceed the safety levels set by the government.

The following two viewpoints present opposing arguments on the issue of whether pollution has made drinking water unsafe or not. Watch for the cause and effect arguments the authors use.

Pollution has made drinking water unsafe

Editor's Note: This viewpoint argues that the pollution of groundwater, the biggest source of drinking water, is a worsening problem. Although rivers and lakes have been largely cleaned up, groundwater grows more polluted every day. As you read, look for the author's use of cause and effect statements.

According to the author, what is the cause of water pollution?

The author quotes an EPA scientist. How does this help support his argument about the cause and effect of lead pollution?

What does the author say caused a reduction of pollution in lakes and rivers? What is the effect of this reduction?

The EPA has identified more than seven hundred different chemical compounds in America's drinking water. One of the deadliest and most common pollutants found in drinking water is lead. The lead usually leaches, or dissolves, into groundwater from lead water pipes or lead solder used to connect pipes together. EPA senior scientist Joel Schwartz warns, "The more we learn about lead, the more we find adverse effects at lower and lower levels. These ill effects include birth defects, brain and nerve damage, and increased risk for heart disease. Drinking water is now a major source of lead for a sizable portion of the population."

This may seem surprising because reducing water pollution has been a national environmental priority for decades. Since the 1960s, the U.S. Congress has passed laws to clean up rivers and lakes. Many American rivers and lakes in the 1950s and 1960s were dumping grounds for untreated industrial and city wastes. Lake Erie, one of the Great Lakes, was declared dead in the 1960s because of pollution. And in 1969, Ohio's Cuyahoga River was so polluted with chemicals that it actually caught fire. Laws have since been passed to help restore these water sources. Now, fish and other aquatic life have returned to them.

"We don't bother buying pesticides anymore. We just spray the crops with our groundwater."

© Simpson/Rothco. Reprinted with permission.

But these cleanups have taken care of only the most visible and dramatic cases of water pollution. There is a far more dangerous, yet less visible, water pollution crisis in the earth's groundwater. Groundwater is the underground water supply that collects when rain and snow seep into the earth. This water bubbles back up to the surface, forming springs and wells. According to environmental writer Steve Coffel, nineteen of every twenty gallons of fresh water used in America is groundwater. Because of groundwater's wide use, he predicts its pollution will be the environmental plague of the 1990s.

Over the last decade, groundwater has become increasingly toxic because it is the final resting place of almost every pollutant used above ground. Chemical fertilizers and pesticides poured onto lawns and gardens, forests, and farmlands soak into the soil. Gasoline, oil, and household chemicals wash into drainage sewers in cities and are carried into groundwater. The rainbow-colored film on every mud puddle betrays the presence of some kind of petroleum product in the water. It only takes one gallon of gasoline to poison seventy-five thousand gallons of water.

Garbage and toxic waste dumps are another source of groundwater contamination. Leakage from these dumps seeps into groundwater. The EPA estimates that only one-tenth of the 80 million tons of toxic waste produced in the United States each year is properly disposed of. The rest has a good chance of leaking into the ground and polluting the groundwater.

It becomes clear that groundwater is severely threatened by pollution—much more than are lakes and rivers. The sources of groundwater pollution are widespread and varied. They cannot be simply shut down like a factory that is polluting a river. This makes preventing such pollution a difficult task. Nonetheless, it must be done somehow—and very soon.

According to the author, what is the cause of the present water pollution crisis?

In the author's opinion, what causes groundwater pollution? Does his list of examples strengthen his argument? Why or why not?

What statistic does the author use to help persuade you that toxic waste adds to groundwater pollution?

According to the author, why is groundwater pollution so difficult to prevent?

A toxic catchall

According to the author, what is the main reason that groundwater continues to get more polluted? Can you think of other sources of groundwater pollution that the author does not mention? What are they?

Pollution has not made drinking water unsafe

> **Editor's Note:** This viewpoint contends that water pollution is not getting worse. People hear that hundreds of chemicals are found in drinking water and so they fear increasing pollution. But these pollutants, the author argues, do no harm at low levels. Government regulations maintain safe levels. Therefore water is still safe to drink.

According to the author, what is the effect of environmentalists' reports of worsening water pollution?

What does the author say is the only source of pure water?

If water is naturally impure, what is the standard for judging whether it is safe to drink?

Environmentalists are worried about water becoming more polluted. They report finding greater numbers of industrial chemicals in water supplies than ever before. Many of these chemicals are known to cause cancer. When people hear that these chemicals are in their water supply, they become afraid to drink tap water. But this fear is needless. It is based on people's unrealistic expectations of how pure their water supply can be.

Most people do not realize that their water is impure. As Kristine Napier of the American Council on Science and Health points out, when speaking of water, pure and safe are not the same thing. Pure water comes only from laboratories. It cannot exist in nature, and it never has. Natural water contains many different substances. Some of these are useful mineral nutrients like iron and calcium. Other substances are small amounts of vegetable or animal matter. These things may change the quality of the water, but they do not necessarily make it unsafe to drink. In other words, impure water is not necessarily unsafe water. The safety of drinking water depends on the nature and amount of the substances in it.

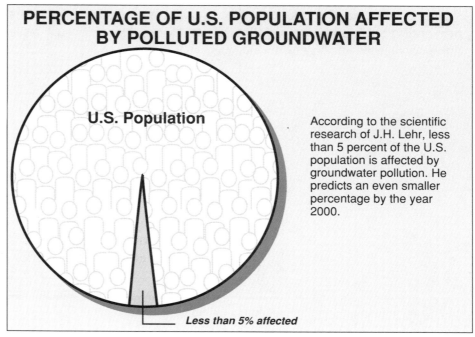

PERCENTAGE OF U.S. POPULATION AFFECTED BY POLLUTED GROUNDWATER

U.S. Population

According to the scientific research of J.H. Lehr, less than 5 percent of the U.S. population is affected by groundwater pollution. He predicts an even smaller percentage by the year 2000.

Less than 5% affected

Source: Groundwater Contamination in the United States.

Modern technology can now detect the presence of some chemicals in water at the astronomically small amount of x number of parts of the chemical per quadrillion parts of water. One quadrillion is a one followed by fifteen zeros: 1,000,000,000,000,000! That is almost like saying that there is one *molecule* of the chemical in a certain volume of water. But just because a substance can be detected in water does not mean that the water is unsafe to drink. The substance must be there in large enough amounts to cause damage. Melvin Benarde of Drexel University's Environmental Studies Institute agrees: "Chemists are closing in on detecting the presence of molecules [of chemicals in water], but does that make the environment or the water supply less safe? Hardly. . . . [It does,] however, create headlines and doubt about the safety of the water supply."

Federal and state laws and guidelines already exist to maintain a safe water supply. These regulations limit the amounts of chemicals, bacteria, and other substances allowed in tap water. These amounts are calculated by determining how much of them a person could consume over a lifetime and still not become ill. The regulations allow a large margin of safety. That is, a person could consume more than the allowed amounts of the regulated substances and still remain healthy.

Water pollution is not getting worse. It is still manageable and will probably even improve in the future. Research scientist J.H. Lehr estimates that groundwater pollution has a significant effect on less than 5 percent of America's population. And he predicts that by the year 2000 the nation will have reduced the amount of pollution entering groundwater by more than 90 percent of present levels. With careful controls and monitoring, America's water will continue to be safe to drink.

What is the effect of more powerful technology on detecting water pollution?

The author quotes an environmental authority. What does the expert say is the cause of public doubt about water safety?

How, according to the author, do governments ensure the safety of drinking water? Does this seem like a good method to you? Why or why not?

LEGAL LEVELS OF MANY POLLUTANTS FOUND IN DRINKING WATER

SUBSTANCE	MAX. LEVEL (ppm or mg/liter)
Arsenic	0.05
Barium	1.00
Cadmium	0.01
Chromium	0.05
Lead	0.05
Mercury	0.002
Nitrate	10.00
Selenium	0.01
Silver	0.05
Fluoride	4.00
Trihalomethanes	0.10
Trichloroethylene	0.005
Carbon tetrachloride	0.005
Vinyl chloride	0.002
Benzene	0.05

Source: *Code of Federal Regulations* 141-143, July 1, 1987.

Pure *and* natural water?

According to this viewpoint, what is the difference between pure water and water that is safe to drink? Why is pure water not found in nature? Why would the phrase "pure, mountain spring water" be a contradiction of terms?

Examining Cause and Effect

This activity will allow you to practice examining cause and effect relationships. The statements below focus on the subject matter of this book. Read each paragraph and consider it carefully. For each one, identify the cause and effect relationship.

If you are doing this activity as a member of a class or group, compare your answers with other class or group members. You will find that others may have different answers than you do. Listening to the reasons others give for their answers can help you in examining cause and effect relationships.

EXAMPLE: Pollution is destroying the environment. It makes the air unfit to breathe. It poisons the water supply. It also makes people ill and incapable of producing healthy children.

   Cause: pollution   Effect: dirty air and water, illness, birth defects

1. Millions of tons of petrochemicals are produced each year. They are not disposed of properly, so they seep into the nation's groundwater. People who drink and bathe in this water often suffer ill health effects from these chemicals.

   Cause: _____   Effect: _____

2. New technology allows scientists to detect ever-smaller concentrations of chemicals in water. It is now possible to detect parts per quadrillion of some chemicals. The result has been that the water supply seems to contain many more pollutants than before.

   Cause: _____   Effect: _____

3. Surface water like Lake Erie and Ohio's Cuyahoga River were once so polluted that no fish could live in them. They have been cleaned up enough now that fish and other water creatures have returned.

   Cause: _____   Effect: _____

4. City water supplies are often more polluted than rural areas. City sewers take in household cleaners, petrochemicals from streets and parking lots, and industrial wastes in greater amounts than rural areas.

   Cause: _____   Effect: _____

CHAPTER 3

PREFACE: Are Government Pollution Regulations Effective?

Government officials have dubbed the 1990s "the environmental decade." Presumably, this means that environmental issues will be a top priority for politicians as the twentieth century comes to an end. Indeed, the passing of the Clean Air Act in 1990 was touted as proof of renewed concern for and efforts on behalf of the environment. Environmental groups like the Sierra Club have declared the act a landmark in the history of environmentalism.

But this attempt to solve environmental problems relates intimately to another top-priority problem dogging politicians in the nineties: the economy. Cleaning up the environment and preventing pollution costs money. Someone has to pay the bill. The Clean Air Act and other recent legislation sends the bill to corporations. The corporations have fought hard to defeat the legislation. They claim to not have the means to pay this bill and still remain competitive in the world economy. Many economists, including Nobel prizewinners Milton Friedman and James Buchanan, are certain that the environment benefits promised by the new regulations will not be worth the stress on the American economy. The $40 billion a year price tag is too much for the economy to bear at this time, they argue.

Nevertheless, the environmentalists won the war with big business over pollution controls and cleanup responsibilities. The new laws are the strictest ever, and corporations large and small will pay dearly to comply with them. The big question now is: Are we paying for a Rolls Royce and getting a Hyundai?

The viewpoints in this chapter debate the effectiveness of government pollution regulations: Do the regulations reduce pollution and thereby improve environmental quality? Or do they bleed dry the nation's economic resources with little gain? As you read, watch for the author's use of cause and effect arguments.

VIEWPOINT 5

Government pollution regulations are effective

Editor's Note: The author of this viewpoint argues that the federal government's pollution laws have effectively reduced environmental pollution. The reduction in pollution has been a direct result of these federal laws.

The author starts out with a quote from an expert to support his argument. Does this testimonial help bring you over to his side? Why or why not?

"Environmental protection has been an American success story— perhaps *the* premier public policy success of the past two decades," boasts William K. Reilly, head of the Environmental Protection Agency (EPA). The EPA is the federal government's watchdog and policymaker on environmental pollution. Since the EPA was formed in 1970, regulations have gotten stricter, and results have gotten better.

Congress passed clean air and clean water legislation. It formed the EPA to enforce these laws. In the twenty-two years since, these

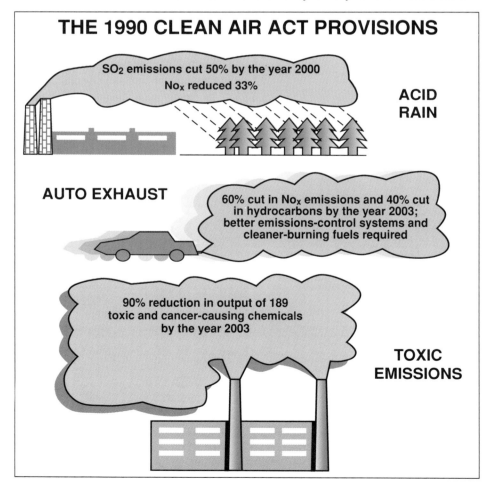

THE 1990 CLEAN AIR ACT PROVISIONS

SO_2 emissions cut 50% by the year 2000
No_x reduced 33%

ACID RAIN

AUTO EXHAUST

60% cut in No_x emissions and 40% cut in hydrocarbons by the year 2003; better emissions-control systems and cleaner-burning fuels required

90% reduction in output of 189 toxic and cancer-causing chemicals by the year 2003

TOXIC EMISSIONS

laws have been amended to make them more effective. The results are impressive.

Today, because of federal controls, America's air and water are cleaner than before and the environment is safer to live in. For example, according to the EPA, levels of all air pollutants except nitrogen oxides have declined or leveled off. The amount of carbon monoxide in the air is down 38 percent. The amount of lead is down 96 percent. Hundreds of water treatment plants have been built since 1970, and the dumping of wastes into the ocean has been nearly completely halted. Hazardous wastes are no longer dumped untreated into landfills. Toxic chemicals like DDT and PCBs have been banned.

These improvements in the environment have not come free of charge. They have had a big price tag. But in the long run, they have, and will, save much more money than they cost. For example, the results of an eight-year EPA study on the costs versus the benefits of phasing out leaded gasoline show a gradual reduction and ban of leaded gasoline cost oil refiners about $3.6 billion. Oil refiners, of course, complained about such a high cost. But the study found that the benefits totaled more than $50 billion, including saving $42 billion in medical costs because people's health improved with less stress from pollution. Environmental damages that were prevented totaled $1.6 billion, and $7 billion in automobile maintenance costs and fuel economy were saved. And these benefits were just the things that can be measured by a scientific study. They do not include less concrete things like the fact that many people will get fewer headaches, cough less often, have less eye irritation, and will generally feel better because they are less stressed by pollution.

The 1990 amendments to the Clean Air Act will also be costly, but the benefits will be worth it. Daniel Weiss of the Sierra Club, a national environmental group, believes that because of these latest regulations, "ten years from now our air will be significantly cleaner." Also, it is likely that in ten years the costs will be forgotten and the benefits taken for granted by everyone. The "hardships" imposed by the regulations will have become just a fact of life. And people will have become a lot healthier.

Does the author's use of statistics make his cause and effect argument more persuasive? Why or why not?

In the author's opinion, do pollution regulations cost a lot in the long run?

Does the author's example of the leaded gasoline study help persuade you to agree with him? Why or why not?

What does the author argue will be the effect of the 1990 air pollution laws? Are you convinced by his argument? Why or why not?

Well worth the price?

The author says that despite high costs, reducing pollution is worth the price. Do you agree? Why or why not? What are some of the improvements in the quality of life that result from a cleaner environment?

Editor's Note: The author of the following viewpoint argues that government regulations are ineffective against pollution. They waste money and put business at odds with government.

What effect, in the author's opinion, do federal pollution laws have on corporations?

According to the author, what are the goals of the 1990 Clean Air Act? What does he argue will be the real effect of the act?

The federal government, through the EPA and Congress, runs the present pollution control system. The government handles pollution problems by making laws. These laws usually make corporations pay millions, sometimes billions, of dollars to clean up the environment. Other laws make corporations install expensive equipment to reduce pollution.

The corporations complain that the laws restrict their businesses too much and cost too much money. For example, in 1990 Congress passed the Clean Air Act. The new law sets stricter limits on the amounts of pollutants that can be released into the air, ground, and water. Its goal is to significantly reduce cancer-causing toxic wastes, acid rain, and the destruction of the ozone layer. These are worthwhile goals. But the cost of achieving this is expected to range from $25 to $40 billion per year—or about $300 to $400 for every household in America! Such a price tag can only weaken an already stumbling American economy. As industrial lobbyist William Fay points out, "Americans will pay the price through job losses and dislocations, higher consumer-product prices, increased electricity bills, reduced competitiveness, changed lifestyles and slower economic growth."

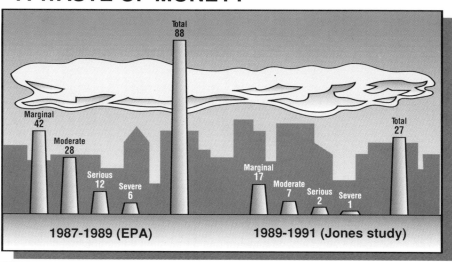

A WASTE OF MONEY?

The 1990 Clean Air Act amendments call for $12 billion a year to be spent cleaning up smog in America's cities. But the new laws are based on outdated information. The graph (near right) shows the average number of cities outside California that violate smog standards according to an EPA study for the years 1987 to 1989. On the far right, the graph shows more recent data gathered by an independent researcher for the years 1989 to 1991. These data show that a dramatic reduction in smog violations was already taking place *before* the 1990 regulations took effect. The $12-billion-a-year cost to reduce smog appears to be unnecessary.

Source: Dr. Kay H. Jones, Zephyr Consulting.

1987-1989 (EPA)

Total 88
Marginal 42
Moderate 28
Serious 12
Severe 6

1989-1991 (Jones study)

Total 27
Marginal 17
Moderate 7
Serious 2
Severe 1

When forced by these laws to pay millions of dollars to clean up wastes or to install pollution control equipment, corporations almost always take their case to court. As Amal Kumar Naj, an environmental writer for the *Wall Street Journal*, notes, "Companies readily acknowledge that it is worth spending millions of dollars on lawyers to put off spending hundreds of millions of dollars on cleanups."

Even worse, many economists predict that the new law will not result in improved air quality or greater health benefits. Why? According to a report by the National Academy of Sciences, the EPA uses faulty data and research methods that give them wrong information about pollution. So the laws based on EPA's studies are inadequate.

Such pollution regulation is clearly ineffective. Its main effect is to make government and business enemies. Businesses spend lots of time and money in figuring out ways to avoid government regulations. The result is that the businesses become worse polluters.

For example, a small publishing company in San Diego, California, generated a small amount of chemical waste listed by the government as hazardous. The company wanted to comply with regulations for the disposal of such waste. A company representative called a nearby publisher to ask how it handled its chemical waste disposal. He discovered that the other publisher simply dumped the wastes down the toilet! The cost and hassle of complying with government regulations was too great. The wastes were not very hazardous. Dumping them down the toilet seemed the logical alternative. Government regulations actually forced this company to pollute.

Public policy analyst Doug Bandow comments: "In the public's eye . . . it is the profit-seeking big business that threatens the nation's ecological future. Yet in case after case, the real enemy has proved to be government." Government regulations have only poured money down the drain in a losing battle against pollution. Perhaps it is time government let private enterprise tackle the problem.

What action does the author say that corporations usually take in response to being forced to pay high clean-up costs?

Why will the new regulations be ineffective in reducing pollution, according to the author?

What does the author say is the main effect of these federal regulations?

Does the author's example of the small publishing company's experience help persuade you that he is right? Why or why not?

Have the author's arguments persuaded you to agree with expert Doug Bandow about who is the real enemy of the environment? Why or why not?

The real enemy

This viewpoint says that government, not big business, is the real enemy to solving the pollution problem. Why is business at odds with government? Do the viewpoint's arguments persuade you that government regulations are ineffective? Why or why not?

3

Writing an Essay Using Cause and Effect Arguments

This book focuses on cause and effect arguments. Authors writing about pollution often use this type of argument to support their ideas. This activity will allow you to practice your skill using cause and effect arguments by writing an essay.

Here is a sample paragraph using one cause and effect argument:

> Statistics show that corporations are the main source of environmental pollution. The way to reduce pollution is to stop corporations from polluting. And the best way to stop corporate polluting is to make corporations pay to clean up the pollution they have caused.

A. Use the knowledge you have gained from reading the viewpoints in this book to write your own essay using cause and effect arguments. Choose one of the two topics listed below. Use at least two cause and effect arguments in your essay.

1. The environment is becoming more polluted.
2. The environment is becoming less polluted.

B. Compare your essay with those written by other members of the class. Write down the cause and effect arguments the other students used in their essays and answer the following questions:

1. Were the students' cause and effect arguments effective? Were they persuasive? Why or why not?

2. Did the students use the same arguments you used? If so, why? Are some cause and effect arguments more logical than others? Give examples.

CHAPTER

PREFACE: Does Pollution Cause Cancer?

"Cancer is for us [Americans]," writes environmental author James Morton, "what hunger is for the people of El Salvador, the cutting edge of the survival issue. It is *our* revolutionary issue." Morton and many others believe that cancer is an epidemic that threatens to seriously weaken the United States, a threat that must be countered immediately. Statistical evidence seems to bear this out. According to medical researcher Dr. Joseph Weissman, cancer is now responsible for almost 4 percent of all deaths in Europe and the United States. A hundred years ago, it accounted for less than 1 percent.

The cause of the cancer epidemic, in Morton's and many others' opinion, is environmental pollution. Toxic residues that are found in food, water, air, and homes continuously expose people to some kind of cancer-causing chemical, many environmentalists and medical researchers believe. University of Chicago cancer researcher Dr. Samuel Epstein notes that city dwellers "live under a bubble of toxic gases." And rural inhabitants live with pesticides, herbicides, and residues from waste dumps. For many, the solution is clear: If the number of cancer cases is to be reduced, pollution must be reduced.

Other people argue that to blame pollution for cancer is simplistic. There are many other reasons that people get cancer, including smoking, poor dietary habits, viruses, genetic traits, and overexposure to sunlight. These people claim that environmentalists are sounding false alarms about pollutants and cancer. For example, Nicolas S. Martin of the Consumer Health Education Council, cites a number of "health scares" that have occurred in the past twenty years. One memorable example is the 1970s hysteria about asbestos and cancer. These scares have resulted in the spending of millions of dollars in an attempt to eliminate certain substances from the environment. These substances were deemed responsible for causing cancer in a number of people. Further research did not prove this, Martin points out, but by then it was too late. The public was alarmed and the money was spent to allay their fears. Martin also notes that many natural substances, including many "healthy" foods like fruits and vegetables, contain chemicals that, in high enough doses, are more toxic than most human-made pollutants. Yet no one is crying out for them to be banned.

The following viewpoints debate the issue of whether pollution causes cancer. There are no margin questions in this chapter. You must keep track of the cause and effect arguments yourself. The focus box at the end of each viewpoint will ask you about the authors' arguments.

Editor's Note: Cancer is the second leading cause of death in America today. The following viewpoint argues that the cancer epidemic is directly related to the increase in chemical pollutants in the environment. Note the author's use of cause and effect arguments.

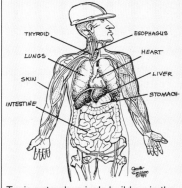

Where employers like to store their most dangerous chemicals.

THYROID
ESOPHAGUS
LUNGS
HEART
LIVER
SKIN
STOMACH
INTESTINE

Toxic petrochemicals build up in the body's organs and tissues. Employees of chemical manufacturing plants and other industries that use petrochemicals are at the highest risk for cancer. Some of the worst petrochemicals people are exposed to include:

Vinyl Chlorides, known to cause lung and liver cancer.

Benzene, known to cause leukemia.

Polychlorinated Biphenyls (PCBs), known to cause breast and other cancers.

Ethylene Dibromide (EDBs), known to cause cancers and birth defects.

© Simpson/Rothco. Reprinted with permission.

"You have cancer." Almost every person living today fears hearing those words. Cancer is a killer. In fact, after heart disease, it is the biggest cause of death in America. It strikes one in every four persons and kills one in every five. Despite medical advances, the world sees nearly 6 million people fall prey to the disease every year.

Cancer is not just one of a number of fatal diseases one might contract. It is, as environmental writer James Morton says, a clear signal "that the life process of humanity is failing." In other words, the general health of people is declining. Their ability to stay well is weakening. Why? People's immune systems are overworked and overburdened by an ever-growing number of environmental pollutants accumulating in their bodies. Dr. Anthony Miller of Canada's National Cancer Institute believes that these environmental toxins cause 90 percent of cancers.

The greatest number of these environmental poisons are petrochemicals—human-made chemicals derived from petroleum. These products range from paints and plastics, to pesticides and preservatives. They end up in the water supply, in the atmosphere, and in food.

Petrochemical production began in earnest around the time of World War II when about a billion pounds of such compounds were manufactured in the United States. Fifty years later, America produces 400 billion pounds of petrochemicals every year—four hundred times as much! And the amount increases every year. Since the turn of the century, cancer has been caused by things like asbestos, radiation, and heavy metals. But only the chemicals made from petroleum, says James Morton, can cause an epidemic like the one ravaging the industrialized world today.

Petrochemical pollutants are effective as cancer-causing agents because they are organic chemicals. Organic chemicals contain carbon and hydrogen—just as human tissue does. The chemicals are usually fat-soluble; that is, they dissolve in oily substances. This means the body can absorb and store them easily in fat cells. By breathing in car exhaust, drinking water that contains weedkiller washed from the lawn into the well, or eating an apple reddened with dye, people permit these toxins to enter their bodies. Stored in fat cells, the poisons are carried around for years. Continuous internal exposure to the toxins, year after year, stresses the body's defenses. Finally, resistance breaks down and cancer develops.

Mike Konopacki: Konopacki Labor Cartoons. *People's Daily World.*

Although these chemicals are present in food, water, and air, the heaviest exposure, says Alexandra Allen, an attorney for the U.S. Public Interest Research Group in Washington, D.C., comes from the air. An average person drinks only two liters of water a day, but breathes in twenty thousand liters of air every day. The air carries toxic chemicals to the far reaches of the planet. Even the bodies of wild animals living in the arctic have been found to contain chemical pollutants.

Residents of big cities have the highest exposure to pollutants. Allen notes that half of the approximately twelve thousand chemical manufacturing plants in the United States are located near the twenty-five largest cities.

Of the hundreds of petroleum-derived chemicals that pollute the environment, the Environmental Protection Agency estimates that just fifteen to forty-five of them cause seventeen hundred cases of cancer a year. If just these cancer-causing killers could be removed from the environment, hundreds of lives might be saved each year. If such pollution is not severely reduced, humans may lose the very ability to survive on earth.

Pollution and cancer

According to the author, what is the cause of the cancer epidemic? In the author's opinion, why do petrochemicals pose such a great danger to health? Why does he say that breathing puts people at the greatest risk of developing cancer? What does the author predict may happen if petrochemical pollution is not severely reduced? Do you agree? Why or why not?

Editor's Note: The following viewpoint argues that the fear of getting cancer from pollution is based on propaganda, not on facts. Look for the author's use of cause and effect arguments and answer the questions in the focus box at the end of the viewpoint.

THE COST OF PREVENTING A SINGLE CANCER

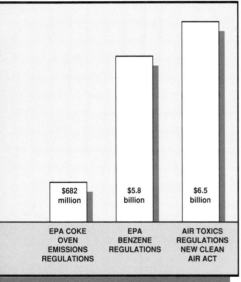

EPA COKE OVEN EMISSIONS REGULATIONS	EPA BENZENE REGULATIONS	AIR TOXICS REGULATIONS NEW CLEAN AIR ACT
$682 million	$5.8 billion	$6.5 billion

Source: National Center for Policy Analysis.

For more than twenty years now, environmentalists have preached that ecological doomsday is just around the corner. Nasty humans, they say, are poisoning the purity and goodness of Nature with their unnatural chemicals. How do the environmentalists get people's attention? Like pranksters yelling "Fire!" in a crowded theater, the environmentalists cry, "Cancer!" No one wants to get cancer, so if people hear that pesticides in their food cause cancer, they will want to get rid of the pesticides. The environmentalists use the fear of cancer to get support for their cause. They have used this tactic over and over again. These health scares are completely unjustified and have cost the public a lot of money.

It all began with asbestos. Asbestos is a fireproof mineral that was used in buildings, ships, and countless other products until about twenty years ago. Scientists found that people who were exposed daily to high concentrations of asbestos began to develop lung cancer years later at a higher rate than normal. Because so many asbestos workers got cancer, someone figured that asbestos itself must cause cancer. So, environmentalists pressured the government to outlaw the use of asbestos.

Studies have revealed that almost all of the cancer-stricken asbestos workers also smoked tobacco. The combination of asbestos and tobacco-smoke irritation on their lungs was responsible for the cancer. The *New England Journal of Medicine* reported that "it remains uncertain whether *any* type of asbestos acting alone can cause lung cancer in nonsmokers." Another important fact overlooked was that the workers were exposed to concentrations of asbestos sometimes a million times higher than the average person would be exposed to.

Similar scenarios occurred with the ethylene dibromide (EDB) scare in 1984 and the Alar scare in 1989. Traces of EDB, a pesticide, and Alar, a preservative, were found in food. Tests showed they caused cancer in laboratory mice. But lab animals used in tests were given very high concentrations of these chemicals before they developed cancer. By comparison, people would have to eat 400 tons of foods with normal traces of EDB in them to approach the

KILLER CHEMICALS?

Many people believe that chemical pollutants in food, air, and water are killing people at an ever-increasing rate. But research statistics show that their fears are groundless.

Trace Levels of:	Estimated Number of Deaths*
Dioxin	0
PCBs	0
EDB	0
Chloradene, heptachlor, DDT (and all other pesticides)	0
Lead in air and water	0
Food additives (saccharin, BHA, nitrites, etc.)	0

*Best estimate is close to zero.

concentrations used in lab experiments! And many biochemists say that the risk of cancer from a glass of Alar-apple juice is eighteen times less than the risk in eating a peanut butter sandwich, fifty times less than in eating a mushroom, and a thousand times less than the risk of one beer!

Environmentalists believe natural things are preferable to manufactured things, but they ignore the fact that many plants have natural poisons in them to protect them from predators. Potatoes contain arsenic, celery contains nitrates, and tea has tannins. Broccoli contains a chemical that, in the human body, acts very much like a chemical currently the focus of a health scare: dioxin. But oddly, the level of the chemical present in broccoli is 20 million times higher than the level of dioxin declared safe by the government! Yet no one has campaigned to outlaw broccoli.

People are fooled by the idea that if something is natural it is good and wholesome, but if it is made by humans it is dirty and deadly. People must become more educated about these matters. Most people do not encounter chemicals in high enough concentrations to cause cancer.

Nature, health, and hysteria

According to this viewpoint, how do environmentalists use the fear of cancer to enlist support for their cause? In the author's opinion, why have the health scares listed in the viewpoint proved false? Why does the author claim that substances shown to cause cancer in laboratory experiments do not necessarily cause the disease in people? Does this seem logical to you? Why or why not? Do you agree or disagree with the author that natural is not always healthy? Why or why not?

Examining Cause and Effect in
Editorial Cartoons

Throughout this book, you have seen cartoons that illustrate the
ideas in the viewpoints. Editorial cartoons are an effective and
usually humorous way of presenting an opinion on an issue.
Cartoonists often illustrate the concept of cause and effect.

The cartoon below makes a point about pollution, the economy,
and health. Look at the cartoon. What effects does the cartoonist
think pollution has had? Who does the cartoonist believe is
responsible for pollution? What do you think is the cartoonist's
attitude toward pollution?

"THE TOXIC WASTE DUMP MEANS A LOT OF JOBS
FOR THE AREA... DOCTORS, NURSES, HEALTH
THERAPISTS..."

Reprinted with special permission of © 1989 North American Syndicate, Inc.

Do you agree with the cartoonist's point of view? Why or why
not?

For further practice on your own, try looking at the daily
newspaper for editorial cartoons. Find some that use the concept
of cause and effect to make their points.

FOR FURTHER READING

The author recommends the following periodicals for further research on the topic. Check the works consulted list that follows for further suggestions.

Sharon Begley, "The Benefits of Dirty Air," *Newsweek*, February 3, 1992.

Gregg Easterbrook, "A House of Cards," *Newsweek*, June 1, 1992.

Sam Flamsteed, "The Hole Story," *Discover*, January 1992.

Jane V. Hall, "Valuing the Health Benefits of Clean Air," *Science*, February 14, 1992.

Richard McGuire, "Economic Priorities and the Environmentalist," *Vital Speeches of the Day*, March 15, 1992.

S.K. Miller, "When Pollution Runs Wild," *National Wildlife*, January 1992.

J. Raloff, "Arsenic in Water: Bigger Cancer Threat," *Science News*, April 18, 1992.

S.K. Reed, "Enemies of the Earth," *People Weekly*, April 27, 1992.

Eloise Salholz, "More Bad News in the Air," *Newsweek*, February 17, 1992.

S. Fred Singer, "The Benefits of Global Warming," *Society*, March/April 1992.

Dick Thompson, "The Danger in Doomsaying [about cancer-causing chemicals]," *Time,* March 9, 1992.

Time, "The Ozone Vanishes," February 17, 1992 (cover story; special section).

USA Today magazine, "Are Golf Courses Poisoning Our Wells?" December 1991.

The following books and periodicals were used in the compilation of this book.

Doug Bandow, *Protecting the Environment: A Free-Market Strategy.* Washington, DC: The Heritage Foundation, 1986. A pro-business solution to reducing pollution.

Melvin A. Benarde, *Our Precarious Habitat.* New York: John Wiley, 1989. Explains earth's water cycle, why pure water is unnecessary, and why government water purity standards are adequate.

Betsy Carpenter, "A Marketplace for Pollution Rights," *U.S. News & World Report*, November 12, 1990. The Clean Air Act's provision for allowing corporations to profit from not polluting will benefit the environment.

Betsy Carpenter, "Is Your Water Safe?" *U.S. News & World Report*, July 29, 1991. Details health risks from drinking water supplies.

Steve Coffel, *But Not a Drop to Drink!* New York: Macmillan, 1989. Industrial chemicals have seeped into America's water supply and are causing a health epidemic.

T.A. Heppenheimer, "Keep Your Cool," *Reason*, January 1990. Criticizes the panic about global warming and the hurried plans to stop it. Believes the climate will change slowly enough to allow people and nations time to adapt.

Richard A. Houghton and George M. Woodwell, "Global Climate Change," *Scientific American*, April 1989. Authors argue that the global warming caused by the accumulation of methane and carbon dioxide in the earth's atmosphere will irreparably damage the planet.

Charles W. Howe, "An Evaluation of U.S. Air and Water Policies," *Environment*, September 1991. In-depth discussion of air and water quality. Includes charts and statistics.

Carolyn Lochhead, "Economists Say Federal Rules May Choke U.S. Productivity," *Insight*, November 19, 1990. The Clean Air Act will strangle U.S. productivity, cost way too much in jobs and money.

Margaret N. Maxey, "Managing Environmental Risks," *Society*, March/April 1992. Balanced discussion of need for ethical uses of technology. Includes discussion of health risks caused by pollution.

Kristine Napier, *Assessing the Quality of America's Water.* 1988 report of the American Council on Science and Health concludes that water is safe to drink.

Robert H. Nelson, "Does Environmental Regulation Equal Environmental Protection? How Current Environmental Policy Is Failing," *Heritage Lecture #376*, March 24, 1992. Discusses how antipollution laws do not ensure a protected environment. Good statistical source.

The New American, "Environmental Fallacies," December 3, 1991. Interview of Dr. H. Read McGrath, meteorologist and aerospace engineer, in which McGrath debunks the theory that the earth's atmosphere is endangered by pollution.

Gary Null, *Clearer, Cleaner, Safer, Greener.* New York: Villard Books, 1990. Claims America's groundwater is becoming more and more polluted from chemical run-off.

Patricia A. Parker, "Crime and Punishment," *Buzzworm*, March/April 1992. Report on EPA crackdown on industrial polluters.

Anthony Ramirez, "A Warming World: What Will It Mean?" *Fortune*, July 4, 1988. Balanced discussion of causes and effects of global warming. Offers lots of statistics.

William K. Reilly, "The Next Environmental Policy: Preventing Pollution," *Domestic Affairs*, Summer 1991. Gives a summary of the state of the environment in the view of the EPA. Good statistical resource.

ORGANIZATIONS TO CONTACT

American Council on Science and Health
1995 Broadway, 16th Floor
New York, NY 10023-5860
(212) 362-7044

The council is an association of scientists and doctors concerned with public health. It works to calm the fears of American citizens who believe their air, water, and food are contaminated. The council believes regulatory controls protect the public from harm and that the environmental crisis is exaggerated. It publishes a series of pamphlets, including *Pesticides and Food Safety*, and occasional special reports.

Chemical Manufacturers Association (CMA)
2501 M St. NW
Washington, DC 20037
(202) 887-1108

The association sponsors research in areas crucial to chemical manufacturers, including air and water pollution. It promotes plant safety, education, and the need for chemicals in modern society. The organization believes that industrial chemical production can be environmentally responsible. It publishes *ChemEcology* and *CMA News* ten times a year and makes available various booklets promoting safe chemical use.

Greenpeace
1436 U St. NW
Washington, DC 20009
(202) 462-1177

Greenpeace opposes nuclear energy and the use of toxins and supports ocean and wildlife preservation. It uses controversial direct actions and strives for media coverage of its actions in an effort to educate the public. It publishes the bimonthly magazine *Greenpeace* and many books, including *Radiation and Health*, *Coastline*, and *The Greenpeace Book on Antarctica*.

The Heritage Foundation
214 Massachusetts Ave. NE
Washington, DC 20002
(202) 546-4400

The Heritage Foundation is a conservative think tank that examines current social and political topics, including the environmental crisis. It opposes excessive government involvement in reducing pollution and advocates a free-market approach to environmental preservation. The foundation publishes the quarterly *Policy Review*. Its *Backgrounder* series of occasional papers and its *Lectures* series of speeches also often cover environmental issues.

Natural Resources Defense Council
40 W. 20th St.
New York, NY 10011
(212) 727-2700

The council is a nonprofit activist group of scientists, lawyers, and citizens working to promote environmentally safe energy sources and the protection of the environment. It publishes a quarterly, *The Amicus Journal*, the newsletter *Newsline*, and a bibliography of books concerning air quality, water resources, and land preservation.

The Sierra Club
730 Polk St.
San Francisco, CA 94109
(415) 776-2211

The Sierra Club strives to conserve the natural resources of the United States and the world. Its publications include the brochures *Tropical Rain Forests: A Vanishing Treasure* and *Bankrolling Disasters: International Development Banks and the Global Environment.*

INDEX